**Contents**

# Abstract

*Deportation of Gang Members: Sub-Optimal Solution for Both America and Mexico*

The U.S. has relied upon deportation as a primary tool to break up street gangs because a large percentage of street gang members in the U.S. are in the country illegally. This paper illustrates how deportation has been ineffective at reducing the spread of street gangs in the United States. It also describes the adverse effects that the deportation of gang members has had upon Mexico, which receives the dominant portion of deportees from the U.S. Finally, the paper draws conclusions concerning the framing of the gang problem and recommends steps to be taken and areas for further research to help solve the gang problem and make deportation a more viable element of the solution set.

## Introduction – The Gang Problem

*Wherever we go, we recruit more people. There's no way they can stop us.*
*We're going to keep on multiplying.*
                                                    - Anonymous MS-13 gang member
                                                    *As quoted in the San Diego Union-Tribune*

When it comes to gang activities, Mexico and the U.S. are linked in many ways. Both

nations have a gang problem. Thirty years ago, there were roughly 2000 gangs with 100,000

total members in America.[1] By 2008, those numbers had increased by a factor of ten.[2]

Although Mexico has no reliable gang statistics, it is generally acknowledged to have a

growing gang problem as well. Most gangs in both nations originally consisted of relatively

small groups that operated around single urban locations, engaging mostly in petty crimes,

such as vandalism or theft. In recent decades, however many gangs have evolved into much

larger entities that operate at a regional or national level, commit increasingly violent crimes,

and have relationships with sophisticated criminal organizations. Regional street gangs

operate in both countries along the U.S.-Mexico border. Several transnational gangs have

significant presence in both nations. Mid-level and retail drug distribution in the U.S. is

dominated by regional and transnational street and prison gangs that coordinate directly with

Mexican cartels and operate in more than 2500 American cities.[3] Nearly half of the most

notorious street and prison gangs in the U.S. have Mexican roots.[4] Substantial portions of

those gangs are illegal aliens.

---

[1] U.S. Department of Justice, Office of Justice and Juvenile Delinquency Prevention, *The Growth of Youth Gang Problems in the United States:1970-1998* (Washington, DC: GPO, 2001), 11-15.

[2] U.S. Department of Justice, National Gang Intelligence Center, *National Gang Threat Assessment 2009* (Washington, DC: GPO, 2009), iii.

[3] U.S. Department of Justice, National Drug Intelligence Center, *National Drug Threat Assessment 2010* (Washington, DC: GPO, 2010), 2.

[4] *National Gang Threat Assessment 2009,* Appendices B and C.

In attempting to halt the spreading gang epidemic within America, U.S. counter-gang strategies have traditionally placed heavy emphasis on law enforcement solutions.[5]  Law enforcement agencies continually seek innovative ways to address the gang problem. Because so many gang members are in the U.S. illegally, one counter-gang tactic that has been used extensively is deportation.  Unfortunately, deportation of gang members is a short sighted and suboptimal solution that does not solve the gang issue.  It merely redistributes the problem.  Deportation has not effectively contributed to the eradication of gangs in America, but it has contributed to Mexico's increasing instability.

## Counter-Argument: The Appeal of Using Deportation to Counter Gangs

> *Now, it's the gang members who have something to fear.*
> - Special Agent Robert Schoch, ICE

With the spread of the U.S. gang phenomenon into smaller cities and suburban areas, there is both greater visibility of the problem and greater pressure from society and political leadership to address the issue.  Many states with gang problems, such as California, have incorporated tough anti-gang legislation that adds additional sentencing for felonies committed "for the benefit of, at the direction of, or in association with any criminal street gang."[6]  Convicting someone of a crime can be difficult.  Proving that the crime was gang-related can be far more challenging.  Moreover, many crimes commonly committed by gangs do not carry heavy sentences.  For example, base sentencing prison terms for common gang-related crimes, such as assault or narcotics trafficking (first offense) generally range from six

---

[5] U.S. Agency for International Development, Bureau for Latin American and Caribbean Affairs, *Central America and Mexico Gang Assessment* (Washington, DC: GPO, 2006), 18.

[6] California Penal Code 186.22. Street Gang, Gang-related Legislation by State, National Gang Center, http://www.nationalgangcenter.gov/Legislation/California.

months to a few years in prison. Once convicted, offenders are often back on the streets and operating with their respective gangs after serving relatively short prison terms. Proponents of using deportation to defeat gangs advocate its use because it does two things that mitigate some law enforcement challenges.

First, deportation offers a fairly quick and straightforward method of removing gang members from American streets. A criminal conviction is not needed to remove suspected gang members who are also illegal aliens. Illegal entry into the U. S. is an *administrative* violation of federal law and provides sufficient grounds for deportation.[7] Second, deportation can serve as an effective deterrent against illegal reentry into the U.S. by deported gang members. Following deportation, illegal reentry into the U.S. is a *criminal* offense that may result in a fine and up to two years imprisonment.[8] For individuals with additional felony offenses, illegal reentry can yield a maximum sentence of 20 years.

Focusing on immigration violations as an exploitable vulnerability of gangs has led to some exceptional coordination between federal and local law enforcement agencies, pooling resources and sharing information to target gang members. Probably the best-known example of this type of law enforcement integration is "Operation Community Shield" (OCS), a multi-agency initiative established in 2005 to disrupt and prevent gang operations and to prosecute or remove alien gang members from the U.S.[9] Under OCS, U.S. Customs and Immigration Enforcement (ICE) is the lead federal agency in investigations concerning

---

[7] Jon Feere and Jessica Vaughan, *Taking Back the Streets: ICE and Local Law Enforcement Target Immigrant Gangs,* Center for Immigration Studies, September 2008, http://www.cis.org/ImmigrantGangs.

[8] U.S. Department of Justice, *Criminal Resource Manual, 1912 8 U.S.C. 1326 – Reentry After Deportation(Removal),* http://www.justice.gov/usao/eousa/foia_reading_room/usam/title9/crm01912.htm.

[9] U.S. Department of Homeland Security, U.S. Immigration and Customs Enforcement, *Operation Community Shield*, http://www.ice.gov/community-shield/

transnational street gangs.[10]  Local, state and federal authorities share information about suspected gang members, which ICE compares against immigration databases to identify individuals who may be subject to ICE's legal jurisdiction.[11]  Advocates of OCS and similar initiatives that focus heavily on immigration violations and deportation of aliens support such programs because they yield results quickly, getting significant numbers of gang members off the street and away from the community, and possibly avoid criminal court proceedings as well.  Such advocates prefer deportation to incarceration, claiming that gang members subjected to the criminal justice system have a strong likelihood of committing further crimes.[12]  Supporters of deportation also claim that the felony offense of illegal re-entry into the U.S. following deportation effectively deters deportees from returning to the U.S.  Since inception, OCS has yielded the arrest of 24,000 gang members from nearly 2000 street gangs.[13]  About half of those arrests were purely for administrative immigration violations.[14]

**The Inadequacy of Deportation: American Perspective**

> *The world is too global to export a problem and not expect it to come back.*
> \- David Brotherton, John Jay College of Criminal Justice

Programs like OCS that rely heavily on deportation appear effective over the short-term when the gang issue is viewed as a domestic problem.  However, this viewpoint judges the effectiveness of the deportation strategy by over-focusing on the tactical victories it has yielded.  If the gang problem is viewed through a broader lens with a long term perspective, however, it is not clear that deportation's tactical victories yield strategic success.

---

[10] Ibid
[11] Ibid
[12] Feere, *Taking Back the Streets*
[13] Ibid
[14] Ibid

In the first place, it is difficult to gauge the real effectiveness of the program even when viewed from just the domestic American perspective. OCS is by far the largest current initiative that leverages deportations to curb gang violence. A perusal of the Department of Homeland Security's OCS website gives some insights into what the program has delivered. The statistics cited include numbers of criminal and administrative arrests, the number of gangs represented by the arrests, the number of gang leaders arrested, and the number of firearms seized.[15] While the figures reflected are quite impressive, they do not really yield insights regarding the program's real contribution towards reducing gang proliferation and gang-related crimes if one takes a longer-term view of the problem. The gang problem in America is simply not diminishing. Analyses provided in the 2009 National Youth Gang Survey yields strong evidence that gang violence rates have continued at exceptional levels over the past decade *in spite of* a significant decline in overall crime.[16] In fact, there is strong evidence indicating that the gang problem has actually grown since OCS began in 2005. "Gang membership in the United States was conservatively estimated at one million members as of September 2008, based on analysis of federal, state, and local law enforcement reporting -- an increase from an estimated 800,000 members in 2005."[17] Gang activity is also more prevalent across greater portions of the U.S. There has been a twenty-one percent increase in the number of U.S. jurisdictions reporting gang problems since 2002.[18] Between 2008 and 2009, the percentage of jurisdictions reporting gang problems

---

[15] *Operation Community Shield*, http://www.ice.gov/community-shield/
[16] James C. Howell, Arlen Egley, Jr., George E. Tita, and Elizabeth Griffiths, "U.S. Gang Problem Trends and Seriousness, 1996–2009", *National Gang Center Bulletin,* May 2011, http://www.nationalgangcenter.gov/Content/Documents/Bulletin-6.pdf
[17] *National Gang Threat Assessment 2009*
[18] National Gang Center, *National Youth Gang Survey Analysis,* September 2011, http://www.nationalgangcenter.gov/Survey-Analysis

increased for large cities, small cities, suburbs *and* rural areas.[19] Admittedly, gang violence is a complex problem influenced by many variables, but thus far, there is not much evidence to indicate that all the deportations have delivered any measurable reduction in gang activity across the U.S.

The deterrent value of the threat of deportation and the penalties associated with illegal re-entry are questionable as well. The fact that the U.S. relies heavily on deportation to thwart gangs is no secret. OCS operations receive widespread media publicity, yet this does not seem to deter aliens in America from joining gangs. In fact, considerable numbers of gang members deported from the U.S. ultimately make their way back to America and gang life despite the threat of criminal penalties. For example, in 2008 during an ICE crackdown across 53 U.S. cities over a four-month period, 1759 gang members and associates were arrested; 1029 of those arrested were non-citizens subjected to deportation proceedings for illegal entry into the U.S. Concerns about deportation did not deter them from engaging in gang activity. Furthermore, another 338 of those arrested had previously been deported and thus faced criminal charges, yet they had not been deterred by the penalties associated with illegal reentry.[20] The statistics in this example are typical of ICE anti-gang roundups: very high percentages of foreign nationals among gang members arrested, to include considerable percentages of gang members who were previously deported.

Some gang members actually exploit the American deportation policies to their personal advantage, and many boast about the ease of illegal reentry into the U.S. along the Southwest

---

[19] Ibid

[20] Cynthia Dizikes, "Gang sweep nets 1,759 arrests", Los Angeles Times, October 03, 2008, http://articles.latimes.com/2008/oct/03/local/me-gangs3

border.[21]  One such story involved a gang member who turned himself in to law enforcement agents,  hoping for deportation under the expedited removal program.  His goal had been to spend Christmas with his mother without spending his own money, and he was subsequently flown home at U.S. government expense.[22]  There are numerous accounts of gang members who have used this tactic to travel home.  For other gang members who are deported, the penalties associated with illegal re-entry do influence their decisions. Unfortunately, this sometimes translates into a willingness to take extreme measures to avoid apprehension.  For example, in 2006, two men gunned down a Texas State Trooper at point blank range during a routine traffic stop.  One of the men had been deported from the U.S. on two occasions.[23]

Lastly, there is ample evidence that deportations of gang members have both boomerang and exponential effects.  Many alien gang members have spent most of their lives in the U.S. and it is the only home they know.  If deported, they will go to great lengths to return to the people they know who still reside there: family, friends, and fellow gang members.[24]  Officer Frank Flores of the Los Angeles Police Department succinctly summarized this phenomenon and the allure of gang life in America when he stated, "The instant popularity.  The girls.  The lure of just belonging.  Suddenly you have 20 or 30 friends.  There's definitely an attraction...   We have seen some who've come full circle – here in L.A., deported, then back again.  It's frustrating."[25]  Other gang members will return to the U.S. to avoid

---

[21] U.S. Agency for International Development, *Central America and Mexico Gang Assessment*, April 2006, p.18; http://www.usaid.gov/locations/latin_america_caribbean/democracy/gangs_cam.pdf
[22] House Committee on Homeland Security, Subcommittee on Investigations, *A Line in the Sand: Confronting the Threat at the Southwest Border,* p. 16 http://www.house.gov/sites/members/tx10_mccaul/pdf/Investigaions-Border-Report.pdf
[23] Ibid, p.26
[24] S. Lynne Walker, "Exporting a Problem", *San Diego Union-Tribune,* January 16, 2005, http://www.signonsandiego.com/uniontrib/20050116/news_lz1n16export.html
[25] Walker, "Exporting a Problem"

prosecution in their home nation; the consequences of being apprehended in America may be less severe than penalties faced in their home country for crimes previously committed there.[26]

The exponential effects of deportation may be worse than the boomerang effect. Deported gang members often influence many other people in their country of origin to migrate to America and to take up gang life. Upon return to their home country, it is exceedingly common for these deported criminals to tell exciting stories of power, wealth, cars, sex, and fighting as part of gang life. Deported gang members are often regarded as heroes who have achieved great exploits, not unlike soldiers returning from combat in a far off land. The deportees tend to portray cities like Los Angeles, Houston, or Phoenix as magical places with many opportunities for improving life if one simply joins the brotherhood of the gang. Whether their stories are told in the barrios or in Mexican prisons, deported gang members entice many others to follow their example, travel to America and take up gang life.[27] In the end, deportation has not been the anti-gang deterrent or the long-term solution that U.S. law makers had envisioned. It does seem to contribute to the expansion of this problem for America, however.

---

[26] *Central America and Mexico Gang Assessment*, p.16
[27] Walker, "Exporting a Problem"

## The Unintended Consequences of Deportation: Mexican Perspective

*Deportation is one of several factors contributing to the expansion of gangs. Deportation... has directly resulted in the exporting of the U.S. brand of gang culture Central America and Mexico. This resulted in Central American and Mexican gangs adopting more sophisticated gang techniques – which originated on the streets of urban America.*
- USAID Central America and Mexico Gang Assessment

While U.S. deportation of alien gang members has not solved the gang problem in America, it has enhanced Mexico's problems with gangs, crime, and violence. It is widely acknowledged that Mexico has a large and complicated gang problem.[28] However, Mexico does not have reliable data on the number of active gang members in the country or on crimes that are specifically attributed to gangs, so the problem can be difficult to quantify.[29] Despite this, there is ample information indicating that U.S. gang member deportations have an adverse effect on Mexico.[30]

The U.S. deports a large number of people to Mexico each year – three times the combined number of people deported to the next ten nations that receive the highest numbers of U.S. deportees.[31] The number of deportees the U.S. sends to Mexico keeps increasing. In 2008, the U.S. deported just over 252,000 people to Mexico.[32] That figure increased in 2009 and increased again in 2010, as Mexico received nearly 280,000 American deportees that year.[33] The percentages of Mexicans deported from the U.S for criminal violations also

---

[28] Max G. Manwaring, "A "New" Dynamic in the Western Hemisphere Security Environment: The Mexican Zetas and Other Private Armies", Strategic Studies Institute, U.S. Army War College, September 2009, p.11, http://www.strategicstudiesinstitute.army.mil/pdffiles/pub940.pdf

[29] U.S. Agency for International Development, *Central America and Mexico Gang Assessment*, *Annex 4: Southern and Northern Borders of Mexico Profile,* April 2006, p.3; http://www.usaid.gov/locations/latin_america_caribbean/democracy/mexico_profile.pdf

[30] Ibid, p.9

[31] Clare Ribando Seelke, "Gangs in Central America", Congressional Research Service, January 3, 2011, p. 9, http://fpc.state.gov/documents/organization/134989.pdf

[32] Ibid

[33] Ibid

continue to grow.  In 2008, nearly 34 per cent of deported Mexicans were sent back for

criminal violations and by 2010 that figure had expanded to 55 per cent.[34]  While not

everyone deported for a criminal violation is a gang member, it is worth noting that the vast

majority of gang members deported from the U.S. are actually removed for *administrative*

immigration violations and not criminal offenses.  Nearly two thirds of all foreign gang

members arrested by ICE are Mexican nationals.[35]  Virtually all of them are deported, either

directly or following incarceration for other crimes they committed while in the U.S.  The

take away from these various statistics is that the U.S. is pumping plenty of people who have

a propensity to commit crimes and engage in gang activity back into Mexico each year.

Upon return to Mexico, conditions that many deportees find there make it highly likely

that they will resort to criminal or gang activity.   In the U.S., the majority of youths who join

gangs are poor, reside in urban areas with higher crime rates, have limited education and find

few legitimate job opportunities.  They are often viewed as cultural outsiders and

subsequently alienated by the majority of the population.  They tend to join gangs for

camaraderie, money, respect, protection, or because they have a friend or relative who is a

gang member.[36] Once deported, many of these gang members find themselves subjected to a

number of the same risk factors in Mexico that they faced in the U.S.[37]  Scores of them

remain alienated because they speak with an urban slang Spanish or do not speak Spanish at

---

[34] Ibid

[35] Feere, *Taking Back the Streets*

[36] James C. Howell. "Gang prevention: An Overview of Research and Programs", Office of Juvenile Justice and Delinquency Prevention, U.S. Department of Justice, *Juvenile Justice Bulletin*, December 2010, https://www.ncjrs.gov/pdffiles1/ojjdp/231116.pdf

[37] *Central America and Mexico Gang Assessment, Annex 4: Southern and Northern Borders of Mexico Profile*, p.1

all. Visible gang tattoos also deter potential employers.[38] Additionally, many deportees are not provided with social or remedial services upon their return to Mexico, which also boosts the odds that they will continue criminal activities there.[39]

While many U.S. gang members deported to Mexico struggle to find legitimate opportunities to improve their life, they can easily find plenty of criminal opportunities to earn money. Many garner automatic respect with local gangs and criminal organizations because of their previous American gang experience. They become prized recruits. Al Valdez of the Orange County, California District Attorney Gang Unit explained, "If you're (a gang member) from Los Angeles or Southern California and you end up in another part of the country or another part of the world, you're considered a big fish in a little pond because you're from L.A."[40] The demand for gang activities in Mexico continues to increase; cartels and criminal organizations outsource a variety of "dirty deeds" to local and transnational gangs.[41]

Deportees from the two most widespread and notorious transnational gangs, MS-13 and the 18th Street Gang (M-18), have an easy time rejoining their respective gangs. Along Mexico's Southern border, these two gangs have established significant presence and control a large portion of the cross-border narcotics trafficking. These two gangs also have almost

---

[38] Anna Cearley, "Deportees are linked to Mexico crime rate", *San Diego Union-Tribune*, September 12, 2004, http://www.signonsandiego.com/uniontrib/20040912/news_1n12deport.html

[39] *Central America and Mexico Gang Assessment*, p.15

[40] Gloria Goodale, "L.A.'s latest export: gangs", The Christian Science Monitor, February 20, 2006, http://www.csmonitor.com/2006/0210/p15s01-altv.html

[41] Max G. Manwaring, "A Contemporary Challenge to State Sovereignty: Gangs and other Illicit Transnational Criminal Organizations in Central America, El Salvador, Mexico, Jamaica, and Brazil" Strategic Studies Institute, U.S. Army War College, December 2007, P.4, http://www.strategicstudiesinstitute.army.mil/pubs/display.cfm?PubID=837

significant control over the flow of illegal migrants from Central America into Mexico.[42] At least 5000 members of MS-13 and roughly 15,000 members of M-18 are estimated to be operating in Mexico.[43] The spread of these same two transnational gangs across the U.S. contributed to America's increasingly aggressive law enforcement actions with a heavy focus on deportation. Consequently, considerable numbers of MS-13 and M-18 members are deported from the U.S. Regardless of where they are sent, these gang members tend to band together "for social and economic advantage, as a way to compete with existing Central American and Mexican gangs, and to survive in a foreign environment on income obtained through familiar criminal means."[44] Upon arrival in Mexico or a Central American nation, it is both easy and lucrative for an individual to migrate to join a cell of his gang operating in Mexico. The influx of U.S. deportees strengthens the connections between the Mexican and U.S. factions of the gangs and solidifies their capacity for transnational operations.

Along Mexico's northern border, the gang situation is far more complex, but opportunities for gang members abound there as well. Larger Mexican cities along the U.S border have significant gang problems. For example, it is estimated that over 320 gangs with 17,000 members operate within Juarez.[45] Operating at the highest level of organized crime in the North are the various Mexican drug cartels, which compete violently with each other for market share, control over various access lanes into the U.S., and freedom of action within their claimed territory. The cartels employ gangs as mercenaries to perform enforcement

---

[42] *Central America and Mexico Gang Assessment, Annex 4: Southern and Northern Borders of Mexico Profile*, p.8

[43] Ibid

[44] Celinda Franco, "The MS-13 and 18th Street Gangs: Emerging Transnational Gang Threats?", Congressional Research Service, January 3, 2011, p. 9, http://opencrs.com/document/RL34233/

[45] *Central America and Mexico Gang Assessment, Annex 4: Southern and Northern Borders of Mexico Profile*, p.5

actions, or to control cross border transportation of illegal drugs and migrants, and to handle distribution of drugs.[46] The regional gangs often use local gangs for retail drug distribution in Mexico and for carrying out various criminal activities. The situation in Northern Mexico continues to yield an increasing number of competing criminal entities. With the fracture of the Sinaloa federation into competing factions, the split of Gulf cartel and the transformation of Los Zetas and other enforcer gangs into organizations that now compete directly with the cartels, the opportunities for violence have ballooned.[47] Thus, a deportee with gang experience in northern Mexico finds a multitude of criminal employers eager to hire his services. Mayors in a number of northern Mexican towns claim that deportees from the U.S. directly contribute to crime and violence in Mexico.[48]

U.S. deportation practices have had indirect effects on Mexico as well. Gang members deported to other Central American countries are quite likely to migrate to Mexico for reasons beyond just the profitable criminal opportunities. Increased U.S. deportations of gang members during the 1990's led to the establishment of American style street gangs in most Central American nations. In response, some nations, such as El Salvador and Honduras, attempted to crush gang activities in their respective countries by resorting to heavy handed (*mano dura*) anti-gang legislation and law enforcement practices, which yielded strict rules and harsh penalties.[49] These firm responses significantly raised the "cost" of engaging in gang actions, which in turn triggered the migration of many gang members to

---

[46] *A Line in the Sand: Confronting the Threat at the Southwest Border,* p. 11-14
[47] June S. Beittel, "Mexico's Drug-related Violence", Congressional Research Service, May 27, 2009, p. 11, http://www.fas.org/sgp/crs/row/R40582.pdf
[48] Diane Macedo, "U.S. Worsens Criminal Violence by Returning Criminal Aliens to Border Cities, Mayors Say", Fox News, September 29, 2010, http://www.foxnews.com/us/2010/09/28/mexican-lawmakers-say-worsening-mexico-violence-returning-criminals/
[49] *Central America and Mexico Gang Assessment*, p.5

countries they deemed as less costly for gang activities.[50] In many cases, gang members migrate back to the U.S. because it is viewed as a lower risk operating environment.[51] Some of those who do not head back to America go to Mexico. Unlike most Central American states, Mexico does not have specific anti-gang legislation.[52] There is also a perceived state of lawlessness in portions of the country. Consequently, gangs view Mexico as a low risk location, and some gangsters migrate there to enjoy greater freedom of action.

Currently, Mexico is simply unable to effectively deal with a large infusion of criminals and gang members, whether deported directly from the U.S. or migrated from elsewhere as an indirect result of U.S. policies. There is compelling evidence illustrating the Mexican government's diminished authority and control over large geographical portions of the country where the cartels and gangs dominate.[53] This paucity of control has enabled amplified levels of poverty, violence, and instability.[54] Current U.S. deportation practices are merely exacerbating the challenging security problems that Mexico faces today.

## Conclusion and Recommendations

*We can be strict to the letter of the law and say these criminals are Mexico's problem, but it's not just their problem because it will come back to haunt the United States.*
- Juan Hernandez, Center for U.S.-Mexico Studies

U.S. efforts to counter street gangs have not kept pace with gang evolution. Once a purely localized problem in only the largest urban areas of the country, gangs have evolved from

---

[50] Jonah M. Temple, "The Merry Go-Round of Youth Gangs: The failure of the U.S. Immigration Removal Policy and the false Outsourcing of Crime", *Boston College Third World Law Journal*, Volume 31, Issue 1, January 1, 2011, p. 198.

[51] Ibid, p.204

[52] *Central America and Mexico Gang Assessment*, p.3

[53] Manwaring, "A Contemporary Challenge to State Sovereignty: Gangs and other Illicit Transnational Criminal Organizations in Central America, El Salvador, Mexico, Jamaica, and Brazil", p. 9

[54] Ibid, p.11

local groups into regional entities operating over a wide area. Many gangs have again transformed into transnational criminal entities that operate on par with sophisticated organized criminal groups. It seems that initially, the U.S. successfully framed the problem as an internal regional or national-level issue and expanded its domestic interagency coordination accordingly. However, the problem has further evolved into an *international* problem that affects both the U.S and Mexico. The gang problem now spans the entire North and Central American region. Deportation has been a significant piece of the strategy to counter gangs as a domestic national problem. U.S. legislators and policy makers must reframe the problem as a regional international issue and coordinate with Mexico and other nations in the region to adjust laws, policies and practices. If the problem is not reframed, emphasis on deportation will continue adversely affecting Mexico without curbing the gang problem in America. However, if changes are made and coordination between the U.S. and Mexico is improved, the practice of deporting gang members who are non-U.S. citizens could become a more effective element of a regional counter gang strategy. The following recommendations highlight some areas and potential changes that could help both nations more effectively counter gangs and make the practice of deportation more effective.

In the first place, countering gangs and their spread truly warrants a better balanced approach. Both the U.S. and Mexico have historically channeled the majority of their resources towards law enforcement solutions to solve the gang problem. Law enforcement solutions only target the manifestations of gang activity, however, so this is primarily a reactive approach that does not address the root causes of gang membership. A multi-pronged approach that better blends prevention, intervention and correction elements is needed. Most successful local anti-gang efforts in the U.S. have employed strategies that balance these elements. During the 1990's, Boston's strategy to reduce the levels of youth violence serves as one example of such a program.[55] In addition to implementing some innovative law enforcement programs and legislation, gang prevention and mediation professionals worked in conjunction with Boston police to help resolve conflicts and connect gangsters and disaffected youth with social services to help steer them away from violence. Specific lessons regarding the most successful prevention and intervention activities from examples like Boston should be applied on a wider scale in both the U.S and Mexico. It is likely that Mexico would need assistance to build the capacity for its gang prevention and intervention programs, but the Mérida Initiative could offer a potential source of funding for this under its fourth pillar of "building strong and resilient communities"[56]

Another recommended change would be to improve the repatriation process for deported gang members returning to Mexico. In 2008, President Calderon launched a new program called "Humane Repatriation," to facilitate reintegration of deportees back into Mexican society. Initially piloted in Tijuana, the program has been expanded to other border towns and provides refuge centers, transportation to home towns and employment assistance for deportees.[57] Unfortunately, few returning Mexicans take advantage of the resources because the program is voluntary.[58] Strong consideration should be given for including a remediation program for returning gang members as part of this initiative and making participation mandatory for those deportees who have acquired a criminal record.

---

[55] U.S. Department of Justice, Office of Justice and Juvenile Delinquency Prevention, *Boston Strategy To Prevent Youth Violence*, http://www.ojjdp.gov/pubs/gun_violence/profile02.html

[56] Clare Ribando Seelke, "U.S.-Mexican Security Cooperation: The Mérida Initiative and Beyond", Congressional Research Service, August 15, 2011, p. 29, http://www.fas.org/sgp/crs/row/R41349.pdf

[57] Ioan Grillo, "Mexico Tries to Help Deportees", *Time,* February 7, 2008, http://www.time.com/time/world/article/0,8599,1710851,00.html

[58] Rudolfo C. Pineiro, "Developing the U.S.-Mexico Border Region for a Prosperous and Secure Relationship: Mexican border Cities and Migration Flows", James A. Baker Institute for Public Policy, Rice University, April 14, 2009, http://www.bakerinstitute.org/publications/LAI-pub-BorderSecCruz-041409.pdf

Improved coordination between the U.S. and Mexico concerning deportees and their transfer back to Mexico is necessary. ICE does not currently provide a complete criminal record for a deportee, nor does it indicate gang affiliation unless it is the primary reason for deportation.[59] A full criminal record plus notification of gang affiliation should become standard information passed to Mexico for all U.S. deportees. A pilot program under the Mérida Initiative called the Criminal History Information Program (CHIP), implemented between the U.S. and El Salvador, yields details on those deportees with criminal convictions to Salvadoran officials. This program should be expanded to include Mexico. In addition, the U.S. should provide greater advanced notification to Mexican authorities in preparation for returning gang deportees, particularly those being released from U.S. prisons. There have been many instances where released prisoners are bused to the Mexican border and freed with little or no advance warning provided to Mexican authorities.[60] Standardizing the notification process that ICE and U.S correctional institutions use, to provide at least one week advance notice prior to returning a gang deportee, would help Mexico maintain situational awareness and facilitate improved Mexican security.

On a grander scale, the U.S and Mexico should collaborate more closely on the development of common regional anti-gang legislation with a goal of creating laws that outline similar gang-related violations and associated penalties. Other Central American countries should also be persuaded to participate in this process. This is a lofty multinational goal that would be challenging to achieve, but it could have profound effects over the long term. If all nations in North and Central America managed to adopt a common set of anti-

---

[59] Seelke, "Gangs in Central America", p. 9
[60] Mark Stevenson, "Criminal Deportees Worry Mexican Border Mayors", *Associated Press*, May 27, 2011, http://www.cnsnews.com/news/article/criminal-deportees-worry-mexican-border-mayors

gang laws that each country applied and enforced, such legislation might help reduce the migratory nature of the transnational gangs and their members. Gangs might become less inclined to migrate elsewhere simply to gain greater freedom of action. The net result could be a more static gang problem for each country when viewed from a national perspective, possibly enabling each nation's domestic gang prevention initiatives to be more effective.

It must be stressed that none of the previously mentioned changes will yield significant results if the borders of both Mexico and the U.S. remain porous. Both countries must take great strides to radically improve border security and reduce the flow of illegal migrants across borders. Aggressive and substantial improvements to border security would truly hamper the free movement of gang members. It would also minimize the human trafficking that many gangs operating in northern and southern Mexico currently find so profitable.

Finally, an in-depth study that focuses on gang member deportation and migration should be conducted to determine when deportation should be used and when it would likely be ineffective. The study should identify the top factors that entice deported gang members to illegally reenter the U.S. Factors influencing illegal reentry likely include the presence of other family members in the U.S., loyalty to gang, profitability of gang activities, and proximity of the gang operating area to Mexico, but there are probably many other influences that might be identified as well. Such a study might also determine whether a gangster's inclination to illegally reenter the U.S. depends upon the type of street gang - transnational, regional or local – with which he or she is affiliated. The results of this type of study would allow law enforcement officials to tailor the corrective solution for an individual gang member based on contextual factors. Ideally, deportation would be a viable option for those gang members assessed to have a low likelihood of returning, assuming the previously mentioned recommendations in this document are also pursued. However, alternative options, ranging from rehabilitation to incarceration, should be explored for those gangsters who are assessed as having high likelihood for illegal reentry. If deportation is to become more effective as a tool, it needs to be used when it is likely to yield a long-term result and not simply because it poses the quickest or easiest short-term option.

In summary, deportation has been a major element of a strategy aimed at solving a perceived domestic gang problem. Thus far, the unintended consequences of deportation have overshadowed its intended effects. However, if the problem is reframed, a better balanced approach is pursued, and cooperation between the U.S. and Mexico is improved, deportation could become a more effective element of a broadened counter-gang strategy.

# BIBLIOGRAPHY

Beittel, June S. "Mexico's Drug-related Violence." Congressional Research Service, May 27, 2009. p. 11. http://www.fas.org/sgp/crs/row/R40582.pdf

California Penal Code 186.22. Street Gang, Gang-related Legislation by State, National Gang Center. http://www.nationalgangcenter.gov/Legislation/California

Cearley, Anna. "Deportees are linked to Mexico crime rate." *San Diego Union-Tribune*, September 12, 2004. http://www.signonsandiego.com/uniontrib/20040912/news_1n12deport.html

Dizikes, Cynthia. "Gang sweep nets 1,759 arrests." *Los Angeles Times*, October 03, 2008. http://articles.latimes.com/2008/oct/03/local/me-gangs3

Feere, Jon and Jessica Vaughan. *Taking Back the Streets: ICE and Local Law Enforcement Target Immigrant Gangs.* Center for Immigration Studies, September 2008. http://www.cis.org/ImmigrantGangs

Franco, Celinda. "The MS-13 and 18th Street Gangs: Emerging Transnational Gang Threats?" Congressional Research Service, January 3, 2011., p. 9. http://opencrs.com/document/RL34233/

Goodale, Gloria. "L.A.'s latest export: gangs." *The Christian Science Monitor*, February 20, 2006. http://www.csmonitor.com/2006/0210/p15s01-altv.html

Grillo, Ioan. "Mexico Tries to Help Deportees." *Time,* February 7, 2008. http://www.time.com/time/world/article/0,8599,1710851,00.html

Howell, James C. "Gang prevention: An Overview of Research and Programs." Office of Juvenile Justice and Delinquency Prevention, U.S. Department of Justice, *Juvenile Justice Bulletin*, December 2010, https://www.ncjrs.gov/pdffiles1/ojjdp/231116.pdf

Howell, James C., Arlen Egley, Jr., George E. Tita, and Elizabeth Griffiths. "U.S. Gang Problem Trends and Seriousness, 1996–2009." *National Gang Center Bulletin,* May 2011. http://www.nationalgangcenter.gov/Content/Documents/Bulletin-6.pdf

House Committee on Homeland Security, Subcommittee on Investigations. *A Line in the Sand: Confronting the Threat at the Southwest Border.,* p. 16. http://www.house.gov/sites/members/tx10_mccaul/pdf/Investigaions-Border-Report.pdf

Macedo, Diane. "U.S. Worsens Criminal Violence by Returning Criminal Aliens to Border Cities, Mayors Say." *Fox News*, September 29, 2010. http://www.foxnews.com/us/2010/09/28/mexican-lawmakers-say-worsening-mexico-violence-returning-criminals/

Manwaring, Max G. "A "New" Dynamic in the Western Hemisphere Security Environment: The Mexican Zetas and Other Private Armies." Strategic Studies Institute, U.S. Army War College. September 2009. p.11. http://www.strategicstudiesinstitute.army.mil/pdffiles/pub940.pdf

Manwaring, Max G. "A Contemporary Challenge to State Sovereignty: Gangs and other Illicit Transnational Criminal Organizations in Central America, El Salvador, Mexico, Jamaica, and Brazil." Strategic Studies Institute, U.S. Army War College, December 2007. p.4. http://www.strategicstudiesinstitute.army.mil/pubs/display.cfm?PubID=837

National Gang Center. *National Youth Gang Survey Analysis.* September 2011. http://www.nationalgangcenter.gov/Survey-Analysis

Pineiro, Rudolfo C. "Developing the U.S.-Mexico Border Region for a Prosperous and Secure Relationship: Mexican border Cities and Migration Flows." James A. Baker Institute for Public Policy, Rice University, April 14, 2009. http://www.bakerinstitute.org/publications/LAI-pub-BorderSecCruz-041409.pdf

Seelke, Clare Ribando. "Gangs in Central America." Congressional Research Service, January 3, 2011. p. 9. http://fpc.state.gov/documents/organization/134989.pdf

Seelke, Clare Ribando. "U.S.-Mexican Security Cooperation: The Mérida Initiative and Beyond." Congressional Research Service, August 15, 2011. p. 29. http://www.fas.org/sgp/crs/row/R41349.pdf

Sentinel News Service, "Operation 'Community Shield' Obstructs Over 1000 Gang Members." *Los Angeles Sentinel*, January 29, 2009. http://www.lasentinel.net/Operation-Community-Shield-Obstructs-Over-1000-Gang-Members.html

Stevenson, Mark. "Criminal Deportees Worry Mexican Border Mayors." *Associated Press*, May 27, 2011. http://www.cnsnews.com/news/article/criminal-deportees-worry-mexican-border-mayors

Temple, Jonah M. "The Merry Go-Round of Youth Gangs: The Failure of the U.S. Immigration Removal Policy and the False Outsourcing of Crime." *Boston College Third World Law Journal*, Volume 31, Issue 1, January 1, 2011. p. 198.

U.S. Agency for International Development, Bureau for Latin American and Caribbean Affairs. *Central America and Mexico Gang Assessment, Annex 4: Southern and Northern Borders of Mexico Profile.* April 2006. p.3. http://www.usaid.gov/locations/latin_america_caribbean/democracy/mexico_profile.pdf

U.S. Agency for International Development, Bureau for Latin American and Caribbean Affairs. *Central America and Mexico Gang Assessment.* (Washington, DC: GPO, 2006), 18. http://www.usaid.gov/locations/latin_america_caribbean/democracy/gangs_cam.pdf

U.S. Department of Homeland Security, U.S. Immigration and Customs Enforcement. *Operation Community Shield.* http://www.ice.gov/community-shield/

U.S. Department of Justice. *Criminal Resource Manual, 1912 8 U.S.C. 1326 – Reentry After Deportation (Removal.)* http://www.justice.gov/usao/eousa/foia_reading_room/usam/title9/crm01912.htm

U.S. Department of Justice, National Drug Intelligence Center. *National Drug Threat Assessment 2010.* (Washington, DC: GPO, 2010), 2.

U.S. Department of Justice, National Gang Intelligence Center. *National Gang Threat Assessment 2009.* (Washington, DC: GPO, 2009), iii.

U.S. Department of Justice, Office of Justice and Juvenile Delinquency Prevention. *Boston Strategy To Prevent Youth Violence,* http://www.ojjdp.gov/pubs/gun_violence/profile02.html

U.S. Department of Justice, Office of Justice and Juvenile Delinquency Prevention. *The Growth of Youth Gang Problems in the United States: 1970-1998.* (Washington, DC: GPO, 2001), 11-15.

Walker, S. Lynne. "Exporting a Problem." *San Diego Union-Tribune,* January 16, 2005. http://www.signonsandiego.com/uniontrib/20050116/news_lz1n16export.html